Doctor of the World:

Poems

Winner of the 2024 Open Chapbook Competition

by

Fleda Brown

Finishing Line Press
Georgetown, Kentucky

Doctor of the World:

Poems

Copyright © 2025 by Fleda Brown
ISBN 979-8-88838-926-3 First Edition
All rights reserved under International and Pan-American Copyright Conventions.
No part of this book may be reproduced in any manner whatsoever without written
permission from the publisher, except in the case of brief quotations embodied in
critical articles and reviews.

ACKNOWLEDGMENTS

"Doctor of the World," *Kenyon Review*
"The Shooting," "Crickets," *Prose Poem Magazine*
"I Used to Eat Flowers," *Plant-Human Quarterly*

I am deeply grateful to my poetry workshop group, Teresa Scollon, Jennifer
Sperry Steinorth, Anne Marie Oomen, Catherine Turnbull, and Ellen Welker,
for their collective spark that makes our poems happen. I'm grateful always
to my long-time and long-distance poetry buddy, Sydney Lea, whose effusive
praise of my poems is probably undeserved but is always welcome. And to
Albert Goldbarth, whose hand-typed hard-copy letters have knocked my
socks off with their devotion to my poems. And always, I'm grateful to Jerry,
without whose love and support, I don't know, would I even be able to write?

Publisher: Leah Huete de Maines
Editor: Christen Kincaid
Cover Art: "Falling Star," Catrin Welz-Stein
Author Photo: Jerry Beasley
Cover Design: Elizabeth Maines McCleavy

Order online: www.finishinglinepress.com
also available on amazon.com

Author inquiries and mail orders:
Finishing Line Press
PO Box 1626
Georgetown, Kentucky 40324
USA

Contents

Through the stethoscope pressed against the wall.

It begins without preamble, without indentation. It is bordered by shifts, like the ritual of fields seen from an airplane. It is not of the same register as ordinary conversation. That much is clear. It ends when it ends, without a moral. It is like a block of baby Swiss, with all those holes. Or a block of wood, polished and set there to be noted and maybe discussed, since it means to catch our attention. It is not song, it is more like a piece carved out of the cosmic microwave background of the universe. Or the sun's solar flares that sound like crinkled paper. You would not hear anything were it not for the scientists who have turned raw data into a kind of poem. More wondrous than beautiful, when you think it has been coming to you from afar, forever, and now it is briefly yours because you are briefly here.

Ridges and Bumps

I didn't know what was coming. There was the big cancer and then the small one. My wild and precious life was slipping out of bounds, while my epidermis stayed silent on the matter. Maybe I was on a TV show. That would explain how things turned on a dime. Where did "turn on a dime" come from? Words start clumping together, and it takes some kind of operation to excise them. Maybe I'm talking about the cancer. If you spin a dime it may fly right off the table. You can't control it. Like "wild and precious life," which of course is Mary Oliver's line that I recently saw in a news story about Kevin McCarthy. On TV, you can change things by giving a rousing speech with "heartfelt emotion." See how hard it is to say something without the clumps of language rising from the depths, eager to help? You wanted to go on smoothly, but there are these ridges and bumps.

The Dawn of Time

The lake's so narrow here that when a boat comes by, it wakes the whole of creation. It cuts a trough that spreads on both sides. When it reaches shore, it swims up the rocks that hold the banks, descends, and returns, each time lower until the lake returns to its base rocking, barely noticeable some days. Water leaves a brief glaze. The rocks and me are definitely wearing away, faint ripples from the outward swell of the universe. The last sigh of the big bang was 13.8 billion years ago. Its wake is the cosmic microwave background. Here come the jet skis, blatantly carving their names, you could say, on the cosmos. It's really fun! It's you! You're awake! You're going so fast nothing matters but staying upright in the turns. Your own fleck of solid matter, everything on earth, is less than five percent of the weight of the universe, but you're tearing it up. It is like the dawn of time, again.

The Shooting

The shooter shot the children. The shooter was shot by the policeman. The policeman was shot but recovered. The cause was not found because the shooter was dead. The investigators talked to the neighbors. Nothing was found out of the ordinary. The brain is not fully developed until about age 25. Fully developed means you might not shoot people. The shooter let loose whatever was firing metaphorical bullets in his brain. He was so sad he wanted everyone to be sad. That could be a reason. What was the reason he was sad? How far back do the train tracks go before they appear to meet? The largest black hole is called Pōwehi, a terrifying behemoth in the constellation of Virgo. This would be the end: a door behind which everything dies forever. If you could see a bullet fired, it would appear to stop dead at the event horizon, and the children would be young forever.

Nevermore

A raven with its ruff of feathers has been hanging out in
Merrie's Market parking lot, hopping onto the electric meter,
pacing in front of the ice locker, a gloom among the emerging
bags of Diet Coke and Oreos. The customers are buying for
a day on the pontoon boats, yet, see, there's always another
point of view, all dramatic and judgmental. Beak-y and black
and certain. I am certain of nothing, so I watch to see what I
might learn. I come as close as I dare without driving it away.
It's easy to be intimate with a motionless silence, to think
you have something of the intangible in you too. Something
uncontrollable, like a compass that knows more than you,
but is you. You can fly if you wish, but you need to patrol
the territory for now, who knows why. It is almost as if you're
loved here, people crouching and taking pictures. You could
make a life of this. That's what you always think.

Cheesy Black Bean Casserole

I'll make the cheesy black bean casserole tonight because I have a can of black beans. I like to plan ahead, although not far ahead because you never know. Florida was drowning, and now it's the Carolinas. No one thought of that. The mind is able to go forward and backward, but it never gets it right. Would I even recognize the bus ride to my piano teacher's studio after all these years? I remember a narrow staircase, also true of the old library in Fayetteville. I can smell the old wood. The future is a can of black beans and cheddar. I could tell you the recipe, but it may not work out as planned. Substitutions are allowed. The weather is always last-minute substituting. It is alarming to live with so much inexactness. The thing to do is not to think about it. You don't want to be like your Algebra teacher, insisting on the right answer.

Crickets

Here are the crickets again, like the background sound of stars. Keep calm. They're no different from your fervent prayers, or the cries in the darkened theater, where you're not responsible. You can say the crickets are singing if you like to put it that way, but the worst of it is that they're unconcerned with you. A thousand bows scraping, a deep meaning you can't read. Leathery wings calling out to each other in the woods. You've never fit in. You're one of God's creatures, yet the angels and imps outnumber you by a long shot. They're out there jumping in and out of your notice like quarks and anti-quarks. Everywhere you turn, creatures have already solved what you've spent your life diligently working on. They're calling out the answers to each other in their secret language

I Used to Eat Flowers

One with tiny white blooms, a little peppery. Even the grasses. I wanted to know everything from the inside. Those ancient little brushes called horsetail. Especially those, bitter, needles between my teeth. Maybe I wanted to eat my life. Maybe I wanted to remember being the earth, while I was still close to it. I wish I could find those tiny white blooms in clumps on their stem. I am still on the lookout. There was some subversion, even then, the slippery boundary of what's proper and not. It's true I still eat a pine needle now and then, or try some tiny white flower to see if it's the same, but the ones I used to eat were in fields that no longer exist. I looked up horsetail. It's called a weed. I am all for weeds, frankly. Too much cultivation makes me nervous. It feels like exile. A deer came within ten feet of me yesterday. It just stood there in the field, its tail relaxed. It was inside my eye, looking out. The wild grasses were still on the earth, and we were still hungry.

Horrible

Think of centipedes in your mouth. Think of roaches in your mouth, their antennae tickling, their little legs flailing. Your mouth and stomach scream "Wrong, Wrong!" to each other. Same when you hear the ones who want to crash the government down. Same when a poem sprawls all over the page. If the poem were in a straight line, you would see its vapidity. The centipede must not be eaten raw. I am a proponent of cooked words, also. Lined up like cookies on a baking sheet. Roasted centipedes on sticks are said to taste like dried spaghetti noodles. Cockroaches supposedly taste like chicken. They tend to run toward you as an escape mechanism, hoping to scare you, which they easily do. They will eat anything, including soap and glue, so they are professional recyclers. China has the most cockroaches. The world is full of things that make you gag, but that's the price you pay for your sensitive taste buds, your beautiful fingers that can caress the tender skin inside your cat's ears, and your ears that pick up her faint purr.

At the Table

I am wearing a red shirt I don't recognize. My hair is still dark. My father is talking across the table to his girlfriend Lois, who came along those years in the summers. Abby is on her mother's lap, recovering from tears. The tears have left a little shine. There is nothing so insecure as the transient world. My father's dead. Lois is dead. I am seriously doubting the past, all that earnestness and tears. On a test, I would have said yes, that's me, but there would be a certain shakiness in the answer, an uncertainty. It must all be true, must have been true! My father in the act of talking, Abby stopping her tears. I am trying to tell you something as mysterious as God. But language is like walking across on wet ice. There's the film of water it gets so you can't stand up. You think if you had cleats you could dig down to something solid. There is a sadness you can't reach. You only know it because of what isn't there.

Doctor of the World

The day before they remove the cancer on my breast, I am obsessed with small things. I am like the doctor of the world. I am struck by the size of the mosquito, the one on the shower wall, for instance, drifting on its long legs, keeping space between its body and the wall, unanchored as I can never be, with my bulges. There are these creatures on the margins, delicate as needles. I also like finding the mushrooms after this hard rain: perfect white, yellow, bright red, mottled orange. I observe that things are so unlike me, so alien. One mushroom floats from the side of a mossy stump like a spaceship. How have I lived in this world so long without being struck dumb? More and more things emerge from their hiddenness. Maybe the earth is showing its face like a last flowering before it is done. Before the waters and the fires take over. The mushrooms are lifting from the earth for a bare few days, saying, "You didn't know what was here, did you?" And the mosquito, living its life on stilts; it has a heart, actually, its blood a clear liquid. The mushroom has no heart, per se, but increases from within itself. The interior can push up between the leaves overnight. It does not know where its borders are until it reaches the end of itself.

Robin

I check on my robin on her nest. I say "my" robin because we've been keeping an eye on each other. B*e careful*, we say to each other, each meaning something different. You can see the waste of the world, the thready nest cascading like a dramatic necklace. What now? I get the binoculars. "Nothing to see here," she says, unmoving yellow beak tilted up like the prow of a ship. I'm starting to feel the way I feel when someone looks straight at me too long with none of the usual banter. Embarrassed, reminded of my body's confusion, stuck forever between animal & celestial. Keep warming your eggs, I tell my robin. As if otherwise she wouldn't. I think I've misunderstood everything. It was those old books on the philosophy of art that said art had to imitate life. That I had to make sure life doesn't fly away from me in the process. How humiliating! Where is it going to go? I'm confused as to how to proceed. I am sitting here as if I were a Greek god waiting for the right moment to transform the living into some grand gesture I could take credit for.

The Trimmers

One balances on the flat top of the ladder, holding on to nothing, swatting at the edges of the huge arborvitae with his toothy machine. He is wearing a hat with a sun-protector neck flap. If you can't save yourself from one thing, save yourself from something else. We are only alive because our sun is burning out, a temporary balance. The burning has made us what we are, one man barely poised, all around the bush, depending on another to hold the unsteady ladder. I can only hold my breath so long before I have to trust the universe to make the necessary corrections.

Loon Cry

I wanted to tell you about the loon that called just one mournful cry this morning, I wanted you to hear it too, the way it pierced the morning and I took my heart in both hands, as Grace Paley said to do every morning, so I wrote this for you. It was a single ooo-w-a-a-a-h-hoo amplified by the lake, asking for a reply or just announcing itself. My words hardly help. It made an opening, a heavy drop of water into water, inarticulate, free, begging for content, for a project, an integration into the present from the loon's far history. I thought, too, it needed to be confirmed in its existence. If I could take that on, the necessary depth, if I could stay underwater long enough to surprise you where I came up, it would be as if I had become disembodied, pure longing, for a while. I wanted to tell you how my thoughts spread out until I was no longer in them.

On My Birthday

This morning loons flew over, crying the tremolo that means this is dangerous territory, keep on going! Is that my birthday present, this rejected feeling? I would rather have morning glories on my birthday spreading their little umbrellas here among the weeds, their delicate persistent daylong pink. I would rather study them as they twine through the underbrush invisible until the blooms. I think of them as resistance politics. I think of the French, their hidden rooms against the Reich. What's held near is most cheering, rather than the ratchet of high loons against the bone. You might say I am unwilling to face facts, the earth burning up, the Cassandra-cries in the sky. Loons have my respect, being strong and ancient and sky-borne. I am glad for their surviving. I want them to keep on to someplace safer, while I try to sort out what to do, being stuck here for now on the mute and blooming earth.

Nighthawks

At the airport café, the man with white rubber gloves pulls the full trash bag out of the bin. He ties it shut and stacks it on his mound of bags. He stretches a new one over the edge of the bin and with a small red plastic tool, punches holes around the edges to keep the bag from blowing up like a balloon as trash is dumped in. He pushes the curtains back in place under the coffee bar with the thermoses of skim milk and half & half. He is contributing to the sanity of the world without giving it much thought. I wish he would swipe off my table and sweep under it. There is a late night mess, but I am working around it, keeping my pizza box to hide the older crumbs, placing my feet carefully. Some people stay put, some must carry things away. The soldiers at the next table are quietly talking, while the ones on the runway stand at attention as the casket is lifted by machine into the cargo hold.

The Hearings

Otherwise there is no sense to anything. What truth isn't is always drawing its excited outline around what it is, thinking you won't see it inside. But I heard, I saw, someone else heard and saw and reported. I can't know if what I saw was what I wanted to see, or if there was an actual event that no one's biased reporting could screw up because it truly happened. Everyone's memory is a little different, so after the fact, all you can do is gather the sum total of recall and average it out. You have videos, which don't lie, as they say, but what the video means is up for grabs. Take a sip of water and answer the question again, your answer will be a tiny bit different because of slightly different words. Still, it will be the truth as you know it, and a thousand angels will defend it with their righteous swords, metaphor or not. They stand at the gate and will only let in the words that match what was inscribed on the gateposts the minute it happened.

Masting

the production of many seeds by a plant every two or more years in regional synchrony with other plants of the same species.

Once in a long while, the trees fling off so many seeds that nothing could destroy them all. Where there were dead leaves, it is all hovering green, tenderly wavering in the breeze. What's scathed or rotten is forgotten, what's raised is bright under the old towering. Just when I could barely breathe, the body electric came to my rescue. Its tiny jointed stems, the contours of its determination. If I thought I had to find a word for the ineffable, to bring it to you like a gift, I couldn't, because it is all shut-your-mouth beautiful. It is smooth and inevitable and overgrown, which should teach me something if I weren't so jerky and will-driven. O history of poetry that flags the dispossessed and spreads them out, too many to ignore, O history of poetry that dives into the dirt, and thrives, all I know to do is climb your roots downward, your inverted tree, toward the deep sky.

Gravity

Today on my walk, gravity kept pulling down, buds kept opening up. Gravity keeps things from floating away. It is heaviness that unites us. Which is to say buds don't open without work. They are pulling up and away from the stem like tiny balloons that think they can keep going, but quickly reach the end of their tether. They feel where they're fastened, which is where the bees want to come, if there are bees. You could say the buds are hooked into a system that can fly away, but not them. Humans are hooked into the same system. We think we can keep on, so the withering is often a surprise. Yet at the heart of our lives is a scattering. This sounds so much like a moral! Like, lead a good life and you'll spread goodness. It is more grave than that, however, more true. Inside gravity is a core the same temperature as the sun. Everything is an explosion, even you.

Muskie

--for Noah

A man caught a three and a half foot long muskie, called me over in my kayak to take a picture before he threw it back. He was holding it as high as he could, its fin almost touching his bare foot. It was a large grayish bullet-shaped breathing, held by its gill. Of course what I say has to stand for what I saw, my words on the page on the verge of success but probably playing themselves out before they get there. Not finished, but intent, the way a fish waits in the shallows for a second wind, a fighting chance. But surely no one with imagination can escape where this is all going, even third-hand. The fish has been caught! What was under the depths, untethered, unseen, has been briefly brought to light, has been made to pose, to show what was meant all along by those foolish, devoted hours.

Clothesline

I am very aware of the limitations. Once I could let things
fly anywhere as if the wind and I had a deal. This was before
I could see the other end of the line. My mother would hang
out the wash. The sheets smelled like air smells if it slams into
something wet enough times. Perfectly delicious, which makes
me wonder why just breathing doesn't smell like that. If you're
at your desk for hours, air quits smelling at all. When I string
up the clothesline I wrap it three times around one cedar tree
and three times around the other and pull hard, which keeps
the small one less bent for the summer. The line is holding up
swimsuits and the tree. I don't like to see a saggy clothesline.
It smacks of sloth. If you have to have two ends, you should
try to make what's in between have good posture. Maybe I
am overly precious about this, but I want to be vigilant in this
job of living. Looking down the row I want to see clothespins
holding things up as long as it takes.

The Desperate Need for Radiance

The sun through blinds casts a soft staircase on the wall. The fan's shadow passes through. I'd be happy to turn like that in silence, performing over and over a mechanical task, if I were not troubled with understanding, and with these ragged animal movements. With so much accumulated knowledge the sludge of it is half lost to me, while the present is like a small child showing off to her parents the dance she just learned. You want the child to be a surprise of light in the shadows of your knowledge, a wild you, a defiant shake at the geometry you learned, against your will, in school. When the sun moves and the wall goes blank, the blind's reflection moves to the computer screen, which just goes to show, a bright story is like an adhesive, with passing clouds.

Astrologer

Don't make me warn you of the stars, too. There is too much else! The water is coming up. The walkway tunnel is already too wet to walk through. You need boots, and then you will need waders. You will be waiting for the dove with the olive branch to let you know there is land left somewhere. You will have forgotten words like loam or shovel. Who knows if the stars will even be alive while their light is still arriving? I don't know what to tell you to do now. Would it be possible to love things frantically, with so little time left? What would that look like, you grabbing me, me almost strangling you, kissing your bald head, your fingers? How would we love the birds frantically, with their miniature twitches? The nuthatch sees from upside down, so cares nothing for the stars. She braces the seed in the bark of a tree and hacks away at it, to get the meat out. She is a little army, going at it. Sure, the stars have something to do with this, from a distance, pulling in to themselves and blazing out. But they're ignoring us as if we were the crazy cousins down the block who consult the Ouija and get drunk on weekends and last week blew a hole in the roof with a shotgun, so now what will they do when it rains?

Cat

Ollie shoves his little head into his little bowl and scarfs down the shredded whatever-meat for today out of the tiny one-serving can. Turns away. Lion. Lion circling, feigning disinterest. Lion in the rough of language, crouched, sprinting across the veldt for it, tearing its flesh, its bloody bits. I would like to feel the rush before, the muscle, the unthinking blur of body, body on body. Something about how language quiets it down, fastens it into pellets, lines them up. I greedily want both language and the rush. I want the claws and the lines of print, settled like a mattress, to dream on. Ollie on the bed, licking his fur. You can watch a cat forever, the soft unconcerned catness, the feathery ears that pick up a pulse of tones, translating into a language forever out of reach, forever not language.

Old Woman Selling Eggs

Consider the Dutch painter Hendrick Bloemaert's 1632 portrait of an old woman selling eggs, holding one egg to her eye (no doubt her sight is poor), smiling a probably toothless smile. She's wearing layers (she's possibly chilled), her head wrapped in double scarves. You might think of embryo (the egg) and age, the two poles meeting with a kind of pleasure on the part of the one who's traveled farthest. Soft light comes from the upper left, outlining the crevices of her wrinkles. She has to check her eggs, to make sure they're good. She can see through them, beyond the delicate shell. It is the intelligence of long practice, of understanding the art of perishing, of holding the preciousness of that-which-is-going-to-perish right up to her eye.

It Seems Right

Chickadees and titmice have paused their flitting to the feeder. Thunder. Now rain softly through the trees. When there is falling, your heart can relax, nothing to do about the falling. A plain summer rain, not flood, nothing washed away, just washed, the way the sky intended. It seems right, the tilt of the earth, sun and moon aligned, clouds wringing themselves out, passing. I wanted to tell you this, to make a shining somehow in the everywhere suffering: that always there is a moment when nothing is wrong, when rain falls on the just and the unjust in perfect proportion, like seasoning, like salt.

Fleda Brown's tenth collection of poems, *Flying Through a Hole in the Storm* (2021) won the Hollis Summers Prize from Ohio University Press. Earlier poems can be found in *The Woods Are On Fire: New & Selected Poems*, chosen by Ted Kooser for the University of Nebraska poetry series in 2017. Her work has appeared three times in *The Best American Poetry* and has won a Pushcart Prize, the Felix Pollak Prize, the Philip Levine Prize, and the Great Lakes Colleges New Writers' Award, and has twice been a finalist for the National Poetry Series. Her poems have been used as texts for several prizewinning musical compositions performed at Eastman School of Music, Yale University, and by the Pittsburgh New Music Ensemble. She has won the New Letters and the Ohio State Univ/ The Journal awards for creative nonfiction. Her third collection of memoir-essays, Mortality, with Friends was published by Wayne State University Press in fall 2021. She is professor emerita at the University of Delaware, where she taught for 27 years and directed the Poets in the Schools program. She was poet laureate of Delaware from 2001-07. She now lives with her husband, Jerry Beasley, in Traverse City, Michigan, where she writes a monthly poetry column for the *Record-Eagle* newspaper. She is retired from the faculty of the Rainier Writing Workshop, a low-residency MFA program in Tacoma, Washington.

www.ingramcontent.com/pod-product-compliance
Lightning Source LLC
Chambersburg PA
CBHW022101080426

42734CB00009B/1446